Original title:
The Coconut Breeze

Copyright © 2025 Creative Arts Management OÜ
All rights reserved.

Author: Giselle Montgomery
ISBN HARDBACK: 978-1-80581-653-9
ISBN PAPERBACK: 978-1-80581-180-0
ISBN EBOOK: 978-1-80581-653-9

Marina Musings

On docked ships, all sails set,
Seagulls dance, making a bet.
Fishermen trip, a splash and a dive,
Laughing loud, they're quite alive.

With salty snacks and jokes to share,
A crab scuttles with comical flair.
Boats bobbing like heads of old friends,
In this harbor, the laughter never ends.

Traces of the Ocean's Breath

Waves whisper secrets from afar,
As jellyfish glow like a bizarre star.
Breezes tickle the noses of fish,
Making them wiggle, their foolish wish.

Driftwood helmets on heads of the gulls,
Sailing by, calling out their dulls.
Crossed eyes and squawks, a comic decree,
Every splash holds a new oddity.

Celestial Conversations with the Breeze

Up on the cliffs, a goat takes a leap,
The wind's chatter makes him beep.
Clouds eavesdrop on the moon's soft quips,
While stars giggle, winking like tips.

Banana peels grow slippery from cheer,
Bubble-blowing whales lend us an ear.
As laughter floats and worries cease,
Nature's stage entertains with ease.

Vistas Beyond the Horizon

Sandy castles rise, then wash away,
As kids in flip-flops join in the fray.
Buckets and shovels, oh what a sight,
Their giggles echo, hearts feeling light.

The sun sets low, a bright orange tease,
As kites dance wildly, teasing the breeze.
With every whim and every cheer,
Joy spills over, the coast's souvenir.

Laughter of the Tides

Waves roll in with a chuckle,
Seagulls squawk, a silly shuffle.
Crabs dance sideways, oh what fun,
Sandcastles fall, but we still run.

Splashing water tickles toes,
Friends join in, and laughter grows.
The sun sets low, a golden spree,
Oh, the joy of waves, so carefree.

Whispering Leaves of Afternoon

Leaves rustle like a joke told best,
Squirrels scamper, never at rest.
Breezes tease with a gentle poke,
Nature giggles, a playful yoke.

Branches sway, a wiggly show,
A swinging vine—oh, don't let go!
Sunlight dapples, a laughing spree,
In the woods, there's fun for free.

Hummingbirds in the Twilight

Tiny wings with a buzzing flair,
Zooming past, without a care.
Flowers sway, a lively scene,
Sipping nectar, so serene.

They dart and dive, a tiny race,
With every flap, a silly grace.
Twilight's glow, a funny sight,
Hummingbirds dance into the night.

Afternoon Delight in Green

Picnics laid on grass so bright,
Ants march in, what a funny sight!
Belly laughs, oh, what a feast,
Sandwiches shared, not a single least.

Kites soar high, see them swoop,
Chasing shadows, a merry troop.
Butterflies flutter, a comic scene,
In the sunlit glow, we feel like queens.

Sails and Shadows

Bouncing in a tiny boat,
With a parrot, my best mate.
Wind slips through our funny hats,
As we chase the jelly rats.

Coconuts are bouncing too,
They think they're in a zoo.
Chasing shadows, lost in glee,
A sailboat dance, just him and me.

Portraits of Serenity

On the shore, a crab, so sly,
Winks at me as he scoots by.
Painted rocks and laughing waves,
Nature's art, mischief saves.

Seagulls squawk while I sip tea,
On a bench, feeling so free.
Suddenly, a fish jumps high,
Splashing me—oh my, oh my!

Afternoon Echoes of Bliss

Under palm trees, life is grand,
Ice cream melts in sticky hand.
Sunshine tickles my sunburned nose,
Laughter floats where the river flows.

Friends arrive with goofy smiles,
We race to swim just a few miles.
But a wave, oh how it pranks,
Turns us over, fishy pranks!

Rhythm of the Island Moon

The moon plays drums with silver beams,
Dancing shadows, silly dreams.
Banana peels on the sandy floor,
Slip and spin, who needs a chore?

A turtle joins, thinking he's cool,
Wobbling past like a funny fool.
We laugh until the dawn steals night,
In this rhythm, everything feels right.

Island Whispers

On shores where laughter flies,
Monkeys wear sunglasses, oh my!
The crabs dance with silly glee,
While seagulls sing off-key.

The tide brings pink flip-flops,
And shells that whisper old tales.
As iguanas steal our snacks,
We laugh at their cheeky trails.

Tropic Serenade

Bananas in hammocks sway low,
While palm trees gossip, you know?
A parrot tells jokes so absurd,
It leaves everyone disturbed.

The sun sets in a funky way,
Dancing shadows come out to play.
We're all caught in a coconut halo,
Hilarity flows like a bright rainbow.

Fragrance of the Palms

The breeze carries a scent so sweet,
Like sunscreen mixed with fried treats.
Cocktails giggle in happy hands,
As sandcastles make silly stands.

Lizards wear tiny sun hats,
Chasing away the chatter of bats.
We toast to a day of pure cheer,
With fresh laughs and fruity beer.

Ocean's Gentle Fan

A sea turtle tried to surf,
But flipped and landed with a smurf!
As waves tickle our toes in play,
We cheer on the clumsy ballet.

Seashells laughing, rolling around,
Jellyfish dance, oh what a sound!
Each splash brings a grin and a cheer,
As the sun beams bright without fear.

Legacy of the Island Winds

In the air there's a giggle, a rustle, a tease,
A dance of the leaves that will tickle your knees.
Palms are whispering secrets, oh what a scandal,
As flip-flops are flung in a wild earthy handle.

The sun plays a trick with its bright golden rays,
While seagulls swoop down making sailors' delays.
Laughter echoes when coconuts drop,
It's nature's own humor, no reason to stop.

A crab in a hurry, a race to the sea,
Waving goodbyes to a well-fed family.
Chasing their shadows while sipping on punch,
They trip over flip-flops, it's quite the fun crunch!

So let's revel in chaos, in breezy delight,
Where the winds have a charm and the day feels just right.

The island's a stage for the playful and bold,
With laughter and stories, pure joy to behold.

Echoes Beneath the Palm Canopy

Beneath the tall palms, a story unfolds,
Where mischief is common, and laughter is gold.
A toucan's a joker, quite full of surprise,
As he wears a bright bowtie to impress the wise.

The sand's got a grin, it's tickling toes,
While crabs throw a party; they've got moves, goodness knows!
With salsa and maracas, they shimmy and shake,
What a sight to behold, what a funny quake!

When breezes blow softly, the coconuts hum,
As if they're in chorus, let's join in the fun!
A sea turtle strolls with a snappy new hat,
Making waves with each step, imagine that!

So dance in the shadows of nature's delight,
Where the echoes of laughter carry through the night.
Let's cherish the giggles and treasures we see,
In the arms of the palms, just wild and carefree!

Wandering Souls in Tropical Air

Wandering souls in the tropics, they grin,
With sandals in hand, they let the day spin.
The breeze brings the tales of grand folly and cheer,
As seagulls conspire to tickle each ear.

With every soft gust, there's a giggle on cue,
A conga line started by a cheeky iguana too.
In the powdery sand, footprints tell tales,
Of wanderers lost in the sea's playful gales.

Lemons in hand, they squeeze out fresh laughs,
While sipping cool drinks in half-coconut halves.
Tropical sunshades shield from the rays,
But jokes in the breeze keep tipping the bays.

So wander on freely, let your spirit ignite,
Join the party of nature, everything feels right.
As laughter flows swiftly through the salty air,
We're ever so grateful for the fun we share!

Silent Duets of Nature

In the hush of the palms, a duet takes flight,
With breezes that giggle, and rustles of light.
Lizards in chorus click their tiny refrain,
While shells kick up dust doing their best to entertain.

When the sun starts to wave, it's time for a show,
As crickets and frogs join the music we know.
A dolphin pops up, adding flair to the score,
With flips and big grins, nothing seen before!

Cactus flowers bloom, throwing shade on the art,
Their petals in laughter, each one with its part.
As the waves join in softly, they roll with delight,
It's a moment of joy, as day turns to night.

So let's raise a toast to this whimsically grand,
To the silent duets of this magical land.
Each giggle and whisper's a reason to stay,
In the breeze that keeps laughing, we dance and play!

Soft Breeze

A gentle whisper tickles my ear,
Palm leaves giggle, the sun is near.
Sandy toes dance on a warm, bright shore,
Crabs in a conga line? I want more!

Seagulls squawk, hosting their own show,
While I sip coconut, feeling the flow.
Even the waves join in a playful jest,
Splashing my buddy, who's taking a rest.

Sweet Freedom

No ties to the clock, just sun and fun,
Laughter erupts, like a race, we run.
Flip-flops flying, watch out, matey!
Sunburned noses: a badge, so weighty!

Hammock swinging, a nap on the line,
Jellyfish waves waltz with the brine.
Our woes are light, like a feather in flight,
This carefree life feels perfectly right.

Journey to the Tropic Heart

Packing flip-flops and pineapple snacks,
Charting a course, avoiding the wacks.
The guide's a parrot, squawking with glee,
Saying, "Follow me, it's just you and me!"

Palm trees sway as we take our ride,
With coconuts grinning, no need to hide.
Every lane's a party, each turn a delight,
Let's follow the sun until it's night!

Harmony of the High Tides

Surfers dance on waves like pros,
A splash here and there, a comic pose!
Fish join the circus, flipping with style,
While I soak in sunshine for a while.

Shells sing softly, collecting their tales,
While dolphins giggle, pulling their veils.
The ocean's a friend, we share our jests,
And in this fun, we find our best.

Starry Nights and Warm Horizons

As the sun dips low, stars start to wink,
The light of the moon makes the water blink.
With bonfires crackling, a marshmallow feast,
We toast to the skies, enjoying the least.

Each breeze carries laughter, stories on high,
While crickets play symphonies, oh my!
Under this blanket of twinkling light,
We laugh till it hurts, what a magical night!

Serene Shores of Green

On the shores where laughter sways,
Coconuts dance in sunny rays.
Seagulls steal our picnic treats,
While crabs perform their little feats.

Sandy toes and sunburned nose,
A drink so sweet, it surely glows.
Children giggle, splash, and shout,
As beach balls fly and worries pout.

Like a clownfish with a grin,
Life's a joke, let fun begin!
With jellyfish that steal your hat,
Oh, wasn't that quite a chitchat?

As sun sets low, the fireflies dance,
We toast to fate, another chance.
Friendship's laughter, never ends,
Here in the green, where joy transcends.

Palms in Paradise

Under palms, a hammock swings,
Annoying birds that laugh and sing.
"My drink's too salty," someone roars,
While crab runs off with our flip-flops and shores.

With coconuts that giggle loud,
And sandcastles, we feel so proud.
Suntan lotion, everywhere,
Watch out for ants; they're hanging there!

The sunset laughs, it knows our plight,
As we munch on snacks—oh, what a sight!
With friends around, no time to sigh,
The coconut fun just won't wave goodbye!

Belly flops and silly tricks,
Our laughter echoes, a magic mix.
The stars peek down, a cosmic tease,
In this paradise, let's kick up the breeze!

Gentle Waves' Caress

Waves that tickle our sandy toes,
While we laugh at the beachside shows.
A hermit crab with such a flair,
Wears a shell, like a fancy chair.

Our beachball gets an unexpected lift,
Smacked by a kid; it's a playful gift.
Seashells giggle, whispering tales,
Of sailor fish and crazy gales.

As surfboards tumble, a splash is grand,
My drink is spilled—oh, wasn't that planned?
Sand in my sandwich, what a bite,
Who knew the beach could cause such delight?

With laughter mixed in the salt-kissed air,
Every moment is a funny affair.
Under the sun, we share our dreams,
And giggle amidst the gentle screams.

Tropical Dreams in Motion

In a land where the sun doth peek,
Dreamers dance, but some feel weak.
With a drink in hand that's far too sweet,
We laugh as we watch our friends compete.

A parrot squawks, "What a fine day!"
As beach-goers stumble on their way.
The sand is sticky, magic glue,
Guess our shoes are now long overdue!

With ukuleles strumming funny tunes,
And no one cares about their cartoons.
Tiki torches flicker with grace,
While dancing queens trip in their pace!

As the sun dips down, colors bold,
Our funny stories never get old.
In this tropical hug, let's embrace,
Where laughter lives and joy takes place!

Nectar of the Tropics

In the sun, bright and clear,
Coconuts bounce with cheer,
Sipping drinks quite absurd,
Laughter shared, no need for words.

Bees are buzzing, what a sight,
Trying hard to take a bite,
But the fruit's too tough to crack,
Honey's sweet, but not a snack.

Monkeys swing from tree to tree,
Taking selfies, oh so free!
They pose with a goofy grin,
While we laugh and round we spin.

A parrot squawks, "Get your cream!"
On this island, life's a dream,
With every swig, we sing a tune,
Underneath the playful moon.

Murmurs of the Sylvan Sea

Waves that giggle, splash and play,
Chasing boats, they dance away,
Seagulls steal the beachside fries,
While kids giggle at their tries.

Tanned surfers ride, a lopsided show,
Falling flat, they steal the glow,
They'll say it's all in good fun,
As the sun dips, and day is done.

Crabs in their shells, they play the game,
Pinching toes, oh, what a shame!
We laugh, and the tide rolls high,
With antics of the sand-boosted cry.

At twilight, the bonfire's blaze,
We roast marshmallows in a daze,
S'mores are sticky, what a mess,
But in this chaos, we feel blessed.

Sandswept Dreams

Footprints trace a silly line,
As sandcastles start to shine,
Buckets fly, a battle's fought,
Seashells scattered, lessons taught.

Flip-flops lost, oh, where'd it go?
It's stuck in the sand, oh, no!
A treasure hunt for things that stray,
Laughing all the silly way.

Sunburns blotch the skin with red,
Sunglasses melted on our head,
We chase the tide, while ice cream drips,
Giggles float on salty lips.

As day fades to a starry dance,
We share our tales, each one a chance,
For fun and joy under the beams,
In sandy, carefree, silly dreams.

Lull in the Horizon

Breezes tickle at our chin,
Daytime mischief wears us thin,
Clouds form shapes, a cat, a hat,
"Is that a whale?" someone asks, "A bat?"

Sunsets splash with colors bold,
Far-off tales of pirates told,
With treasure maps that never lead,
To places where dreams plant their seed.

Starry nights, we fish with style,
Reeling thoughts that make us smile,
But often it's the fish that win,
They laugh and watch, while we chagrin.

And as the moon begins to rise,
We sit and gaze with sleepy eyes,
With echoes of the day behind,
A funny world is what we find.

Ephemeral Island Wonders

A coconut rolled by, oh what a sight,
It cracked on my head, gave me quite a fright.
The seagulls all laughed, they flapped with glee,
As I searched for my hat in the palm of a tree.

The waves danced around in a giggling spree,
Shells whispered secrets, just for me.
But first, I tripped over a flip-flop pair,
And landed face-first in sand without a care!

A crab scuttled by with a swagger so bold,
He winked as he passed, or so I was told.
I followed his lead, did a little jig,
Until my dance partner—a coconut—got big!

So here's to the beach, where slapstick abounds,
Where laughter and coconuts put joy in the rounds.
I'll laugh till I cry, as the sun starts to fade,
In this whimsical land, my worries will jade.

Dreams on a Gentle Tide

Under the sun, I decided to play,
With a beach ball that wandered a little away.
It rolled in the surf, I chased with a cheer,
But it floated off like my hopes for the year!

A dolphin swam by, with a wink and a flip,
I tried to impress, but I fell on my hip.
The waves laughed aloud, with a splash and a roar,
As I rolled on the sand, saying, 'Hey, that's not sore!'

The crabs held a conference, they plotted with flair,
Wearing shells as their hats, discussing my dare.
I borrowed their moves, tried a crabby old strut,
They clapped with their claws, then said I was nuts!

But here in the sun, every tumble's a gift,
With sand in my hair and my spirits to lift.
So I'll dance on the shore with the waves as my beat,
In dreams on a tide, life's bittersweet treat.

Salted Air Symphony

Salty curls swirl up with glee,
As seagulls squawk a jolly spree.
Waves dance like they've lost their mind,
In this chaos, laughs we find.

Kites snagging in coconut trees,
Chasing tales on a restless breeze.
Flip-flops flung in a wild jest,
To take off is the ultimate quest.

Evening Currents of Bliss

Sunset paints the sky in hues,
While sandcastles become our muse.
Laughter echoes in the twilight,
As beach balls soar, oh what a sight!

With a wink, the waves come near,
Chasing dreams, we dance and cheer.
Ice cream drips on a playful grin,
The fun has only just begun!

Paradise's Soft Embrace

Coconuts wobble, round and sweet,
Tickling toes in the sandy heat.
With each gulp of sun-kissed air,
A corny joke floats—who can compare?

Hammocks sway, a gentle tease,
Where snores join in the rustling trees.
Frolicking friends in colorful attire,
Spread laughter like sweet confetti fire.

Breezy Liaisons

Tangled hair and carefree shouts,
Where evening brings mischief in bouts.
Smoothie spills and goofy falls,
Crafting smiles in ocean stalls.

A crab plays tag; the crowd is wild,
Like a group of giggling children styled.
With each wave, new jokes unfold,
In this paradise, we're never old.

Songs of Sand and Shell

On the beach, where footprints dance,
A crab in shorts takes a chance.
Shells sing tunes, a merry crew,
They rock like boats, just me and you.

Seagulls squawk, they steal my fries,
Winking at the sun, they rise.
Sandcastles toppled by a wave,
A sandy king, oh, how they rave!

Flip-flops flapping, shoes misplaced,
Chasing sand, a wild rat race.
Laughter mixes with the tide,
In this joy, we all abide.

With every wave, a funny tale,
Stories of fish, and silly whales.
Under palm trees, grass skirts sway,
We dance like no one's watching, hey!

Rafting Rhythm of the Isle

In a blow-up boat, we start to glide,
Paddling hard, what a goofy ride!
A splash here, a splash there, oh dear,
Fully soaked, collecting cheer.

Fish peek up, give us a show,
Their tiny laughs, we surely know.
Waves carry jokes, a bubbly sound,
Floating on laughter, bliss we found.

The sun's a spotlight, it's got no shame,
It's roasting us, oh, what a game!
A crab on board, he steals our snack,
With a sideways grin, he won't look back.

As we paddle in circles, round and round,
Our silly adventures echo in sound.
With splashes and giggles, we drift along,
Making memories where we belong.

Morning Hope and Evening Gold

Morning sun, a playful tease,
It tickles waves, dances with ease.
Breezy whispers, a sweet surprise,
Sand dunes rolling like happy pies.

Coffee cups held high with cheer,
Birds join in, we start to hear.
Laughter rises with each new ray,
Chasing clouds that run away!

Evening settles, colors blend,
We giggle softly as day will end.
A beach ball rolls, a fitful chat,
Wait—who brought an inflatable cat?

As the stars twinkle, we reminisce,
Each memory wrapped in sandy bliss.
With neon glow sticks, we're on a roll,
Dancing till dawn, that's our goal!

Cascading Waves of Delight

Waves tumble down in a comedy show,
Each bubble pops, now where will they go?
Surfboards wobble, a clumsy parade,
As laughter erupts, not a moment's fade.

The lifeguard snoozes, dreaming of snacks,
While a flock of ducks navigates the tracks.
They quack in rhythm, a silly tune,
Join their chorus, 'neath the bright moon.

Footprints in sand, a messy design,
With every giggle, our spirits align.
The tide pulls back, leaving us glee,
As we sculpt a shark, come share with me!

In the midst of joy, we find our way,
Happiness flows like the waves at play.
So grab your friends, come take a dip,
In cascading fun, let laughter rip!

Unwritten Verses of the Isle

On a lonesome beach towel lay,
A seagull stole my sandwich today.
I chased it round with a splash and a scream,
While my friends all laughed like it's part of a dream.

A crab did a dance on the hot, soft sand,
I tried to join in; it did not go as planned.
With pinchers raised high, it gave me a fright,
I learned the hard way, crabs don't share stage light.

A parrot squawks jokes to the waves and the sky,
While I'm just here wondering why I can't fly.
The birds roll their eyes, like they know I'm a fool,
As I attempt to surf on a well-worn pool noodle.

At sunset we gather, the stories take flight,
With laughter and giggles, our worries take flight.
Beneath the moon's glow, with mirth in the air,
We write unwritten verses, with not a single care.

Coconuts and Sunbeams

The coconuts tumble, like little round balls,
They roll down the shore, bouncing off the sea walls.
We laugh as we dive, trying to catch them in time,
Only to find jellyfish dance in their prime.

Sunbeams giggle as they peek through the trees,
While we try to dodge the honeybees' tease.
With flip-flops in hand, we take on the land,
Running from shadows, it's all quite unplanned.

A toucan whispers a secret so sly,
It calls me a monkey; I can't even lie!
I swing from a branch, with a laugh and a cheer,
But slip on a banana—oh dear, oh dear!

As nightfall arrives, the stars start to play,
We gather around, in our own quirky way.
With jokes and with stories, we'll dance 'til it's bright,
Under the glow of the moon, what a hilarious sight!

Secrets of the Soft Wind

The soft wind whispers, with giggles and cheer,
It tells me my hairstyle is quite the wild deer.
I run from the brush, with a hat on my face,
Hoping the breeze will change with its pace.

Palm trees are swaying, like dancers on cue,
They twist and they twirl, in a wacky review.
I join in the frolic, arms flapping like sails,
But trip on some roots, losing all of my trails.

A dog on the far side joins in on the fun,
He chases after birds; oh look, there he runs!
We laugh as he tumbles, right into a puddle,
A splash of confusion, oh, what a muddle!

As twilight arrives, we gather and grieve,
For those silly moments, it's hard to believe.
With secrets of winds, soft and laid back,
We hold onto laughter as the sun starts to crack.

Nature's Gentle Serenade

The waves sing a tune as they crash on the shore,
While I trip over sandals, who could ask for more?
A jellyfish giggles, swaying in rhythm,
It can't help but laugh at my ridiculous schism.

The tide comes in softly, like a sweet lullaby,
But I'm busy tripping, oh my, oh my!
With sand in my shoes and a grin on my face,
I chase after crabs, keeping up with their pace.

Beneath the palm trees, our hearts start to dance,
As the night creeps in, we embrace the chance.
With fireflies twinkling, we sing in delight,
For nothing's more funny than nature's goodnight.

With friends all around, we laugh at our flaws,
Celebrating the evening, clapping our paws.
In nature's sweet serenade, we find our own tune,
As laughter echoes softly beneath the bright moon.

Ocean Mist and Coconut Dreams

In the haze of the salty air,
Coconuts roll without a care,
Seagulls sneak on sandy ground,
Nabbing snacks, they squawk around.

Tropical drinks with tiny straws,
Splashing juice, we laugh because,
A sip too much, and here we sway,
Daring waves come out to play.

The ukulele strums a tune,
While crabs attempt a silly moon,
Dance in rhythm, claw and grin,
What a show, let the fun begin!

Mango floats become our shields,
Defense against the wild yard fields,
With friends beside, how could we tire?
Each chuckle is a heart's desire.

Sunlit Pathways of Paradise

Sunlight dances on the sea,
Crabs in suits as bold can be,
Flip flops squeak, and we all race,
Dodging waves, a slapstick chase.

Salty snacks and splashes fly,
Fish dive deep, they wonder why,
Every cast brings laughter loud,
As we celebrate and feel proud.

Life's a treasure hunt on shore,
Finding seashells, want some more,
A crab on my foot steals the show,
Wiggling sideways, watch it go!

Picnic baskets spill and sway,
As seagulls plot their grand buffet,
Up we jump with forks in hand,
A feast, a fishy, flaky band!

Sun-Kissed Moments

Under the sun, we all collide,
Coconut hats the latest pride,
Splashing water, oh what a scene,
Colorful chaos, looking keen!

Towels tossed in a flutter breeze,
Laughter rings through palm tree leaves,
Sand stuck on toes, our little plight,
Making memories in pure daylight.

The ice cream truck honks, oh yay,
Hurrying feet join in the play,
Cone in hand, I take a chance,
Dripping goo, the wobbly dance!

Waves retreat, we cheer and roam,
Finding shells, our treasure home,
Each giggle adds to the delight,
Sun-kissed moments feel so right!

Tranquil Waters and Swaying Palms

Palm trees wiggle in the sun,
While locals joke and have their fun,
A lizard slips on a timepiece,
Laughing hard, it won't cease!

The water glistens, what a sight,
A fish pops up – oh what a fright,
Jumping high just to escape,
With scales that shimmer like a cape!

Beachcombers stumble on their quest,
Finding treasures, oh the jest,
Friends in buckets, what a mess,
Sandy hats in sheer excess!

Sunset fades, bright colors blend,
With silly stories, laughter sends,
A day of joy, we leave our mark,
Grateful for each giggly spark.

Melodies of the Tropic Nights

A coconut fell right on my head,
I laughed so hard, I nearly fled.
Dance with shadows, stomp your feet,
Drinks in hand, oh what a treat!

The crabs are grooving on the sand,
In tiny tuxedos, they make their stand.
With every wave, they take a bow,
I'd dance like them, but not right now!

A parrot squawks a silly song,
While I try my best to sing along.
Beachcomber hat on my brow,
Ladies and gents, take your vows!

Nights filled with laughter and surprise,
As stars twinkle in the skies.
With a wink and a sway, we play,
In tropic joy, we shall stay!

Chasing the Horizon

I tried to catch a wave one day,
But fell instead in a funny way.
With sand in shorts and a goofy grin,
I'll do it all again, with a spin!

The boat tipped over, oh what fun!
We splashed around like kids on the run.
Flip-flops flying through the air,
Who knew a boat ride could be a dare?

Seagulls cackled at our plight,
As we tried to get our grip right.
With watermelon juice in tow,
We ventured on, a funny show!

Chasing sunsets, we're a sight,
Dancing under the moonlight!
With joy like a red balloon,
Oh, nothing's better than this tune!

Breeze-Kissed Reveries

A gentle tickle from the breeze,
As I attempt to climb the trees.
With coconuts as my best pals,
I'm on an adventure, plotting our gales!

Fruits tumble down, making a mess,
Should I worry? Nah, I confess!
Barefoot chaos, laughter ignites,
Chasing dreams in the warm moonlight.

The hammock swings, it's quite a feat,
I slide right off, what a defeat!
Launching myself like a cannonball,
At least I've got that coconut haul!

The sun sets low in giggles and grins,
With friends around, how the fun begins!
Flipping pancakes made of sand,
In this magical, funny land!

Sunsets over Palm Groves

Oh, the palm shades are such a tease,
I swear they giggle in the breeze.
I stumble, trip over my toes,
Finding balance is how it goes!

Sunset colors make it bright,
While I aimlessly wander, pure delight.
Caught in laughter, the sky ablaze,
Like a child lost in a playful maze!

Ice cream drips down my hand,
As I chase flavors in this land.
The night calls out with cozy cheer,
Who knew fun would be so near?

So let's toast with fruity drinks,
As the sun winks and the ocean blinks.
With funny stories we'll regale,
Under twilight, we shall prevail!

Isles of Tranquility

On sandy shores where crabs do dance,
They sidestep grace, in a funny prance.
With flower crowns upon their heads,
They sip on drinks made out of threads.

A parrot squawks with quite the flair,
While turtles race without a care.
With coconut hats and giant laughs,
They discuss why time's slow with the gaffs.

Beach balls bounce with laughter loud,
As kids build castles, tall and proud.
But waves, they scheme, with frothy grins,
And sweep away their moisty wins.

As night descends, the stars appear,
A crab tells jokes, the crowd will cheer.
In this paradise, fun runs high,
With silliness beneath the sky.

Cascades of Whispering Winds

A zephyr blows like mischief's hand,
It tickles toes upon the sand.
With umbrellas flying every way,
They dance and spin, come join the play.

The sunburnt folks, they start to roast,
While seagulls laugh, they love to boast.
A stumble here, a slip right there,
The beach is filled with joyful scare.

A frisbee flies, it ricochets,
Smashing drinks and cakes that wait.
And laughter rings as splashes fly,
Outrageous fun, oh me, oh my!

As dusk arrives, the grill ignites,
With funny tales and goofy fright.
A serenade of goofy tunes,
As stars above sway like buffoons.

Maritime Reveries

The ocean calls with a giggle sound,
As fishermen toss, their lines abound.
With jokes that sink, and laughter floats,
   They reel in tales, not just in boats.

The shrimp debate who's best to eat,
While crabs form bands in their retreat.
With snares of laughter, they conspire,
   To give the tourists quite the ire.

A dolphin jumps, performs a twist,
While kids, they squeal, they can't resist.
With goggles on, they dive for fun,
Only to find seaweed, tons of none.

As twilight dims, the sailboats sway,
With tales of fish that got away.
In maritime dreams, let laughter reign,
For at the sea, there's joy to gain.

Allure of the Ocean's Edge

At sunrise bright, the ocean quips,
While surfers tumble, take their dips.
With salty snacks and blender swirls,
They ride the waves, like silly pearls.

A crab with shades tries to assert,
He's cooler than the sun-kissed shirt.
With dance moves that would make one cringe,
He rallies all for one wild binge.

The tides roll in, a playful foe,
As beachgoers dodge the goofy flow.
With sandcastles that start to lean,
Funny faces fill the scene, obscene.

As night unfolds, the lanterns glow,
With jokes that sprinkle like a show.
Laughter echoes, joy finds a wedge,
In comedic bliss at the ocean's edge.

Dancing Leaves of Summer

Underneath the sun's tight grasp,
Leaves twirl like dancers with a gasp.
Grasshoppers leap, a whimsical bunch,
Inviting bugs to join the lunch.

Sweat beads roll, oh what a treat,
Bikini tops, and flip-flops sweet.
Kids laugh loud, the ice cream's here,
Sling it fast, or feel the fear!

Squirrels mock with cheeky chitter,
As birds join in - does the sun ever glitter?
Crickets pitch in with tuneful glee,
Nature's orchestra, silly as can be!

But watch your hats, the breeze is sly,
It lifts and swirls, oh my, oh my!
Dancing leaves, both high and low,
Keep up the fun, or off they go!

Echoes of the Ocean's Song

Waves crash down in a playful roar,
Seagulls swoop, then dance on the shore.
Shells giggle softly as they roll,
The tide's a jester, with a frothy control.

Sunburned backs and sandy toes,
Crabs in tuxedos, oh look how they pose!
Beach balls bouncing, laughter in flight,
The ocean whispers jokes every night.

Old fishermen spin tales of the deep,
While toddlers stumble, and parents leap.
Nets full of fish and a bucket of fun,
Clams play tag while the day's nearly done.

As twilight creeps, and stars arise,
The moon winks down with playful sighs.
Waves continue their ticklish tease,
In this shore's embrace, we glide with ease.

Swaying Palms and Rhythmic Tides

Palms sway slow with a funky beat,
Thumping like a heart, oh what a treat!
With coconuts bobbing in bright sunlight,
And critters wearing shades, it's quite the sight.

The sea frolics, splashes all around,
Bananas float by, oh what a sound!
Laughter erupts from sandy toes,
As kites take flight where the warm wind blows.

Surfboards standing in a line so neat,
Silly surfers try to stay on their feet.
Flip-flops flying, they conquer the waves,
While seagulls swoop for the crumbs they crave.

A conch calls out with zestful cheer,
Drawing folks close as night time nears.
Under the moon, we all dance free,
Palm trees sway like it's a jubilee!

A Symphony of Island Scents

The air is thick with fruity bliss,
Mango tango, who could resist?
Pineapple whirls in a tropical dance,
While coconuts nod, losing their stance.

Spices sizzle with a burst of delight,
Fish grilling high under stars so bright.
Roasting marshmallows - a toasty cheer,
As laughter erupts, draw close my dear!

The scent of coconut wraps around,
Like a cheeky hug that twirls around.
Herbs whisper sweet tunes through the night,
While fireflies flash in a wiggly flight.

But beware of the onions, that's a true trap,
One sniff too close could lead to a nap!
With giggles and grins, we'll solve this quest,
For this island feast surely is the best!

Sand and Sea's Eloquent Dance

Waves are clumsy, tripping high,

Seagulls squawking, oh my, oh my.
Sandcastles wobble, collapse with glee,
It's a beach party, come join me!

Flip-flops flying, lost in flight,
A crab in shades, what a sight!
Tanned tourists sunbathe, snoring loud,
While a dog steals lunch from the crowd.

Beach balls bouncin' in the air,
Jellyfish seem to dance with care.
Tiki torches light up the dark,
As we laugh at that walrus' bark.

Seashells giggle in the sun's glow,
Tiny creatures are putting on a show.
With every splash, we dance with joy,
The sand and sea, our silly toy!

Embrace of the Gentle Tide

The tide rolls in, then rolls back out,
A soggy sock brings squeals and shouts.
Paddling feet, laughter everywhere,
Oh look! A beach ball flying through air!

Pineapple drinks go straight to our heads,
We sip and spill, making funny threads.
The breeze teases hair, wild and free,
We chase crabs, as they flee from me!

Surfboards wobble, balancing grace,
As the ocean decides to give chase.
We tumble and laugh, drenched to the bone,
Like silly seals, we play on our own.

Sunburnt noses, a rosy hue,
Tell funny tales, both old and new.
In the embrace of the gentle tide,
Laughter and waves go side by side!

Serenade of the Coastal Breeze

A mango falls, what a surprise,
As squirrels plot from the treetops high.
Wind plays tricks, it won't behave,
Sending hats sailing, oh how they wave!

Beach umbrellas dance a little jig,
As if it's the silliest gig.
Sandy toes squish with every step,
A treasure chest, oh where's the rep?

Crabs wearing shells like tiny hats,
Prance around, avoiding spry cats.
Waves tap-dance, a show on the shore,
Making us giggle, then laugh some more.

With playful winds and skies so blue,
This coastal serenade sings to you.
Come join the fun, in nature's now,
As laughter rings through the salty vow!

Kaleidoscope of Island Colors

Sunsets splash like paint on a canvas,
Pinky skies framed with coconut madness.
Flamboyant flowers wave hello,
In this joyful place where breezes flow.

Beachgoers wear the wildest wigs,
As hula dancers show off their digs.
Laughter blends with the ocean's roar,
Colors whirl in a sunny encore.

Fish in stripes, all around us flash,
While hermit crabs join in with a dash.
Mismatched flip-flops on toes galore,
We trip and tumble, falling on the shore.

Under the shade, we savor each bite,
Of ice cream cones that melt, what a sight!
With each bright laugh, we paint the day,
In a kaleidoscope, we dance and play!

Sunlit Shores' Lullaby

On sandy shores where seagulls play,
A crab decided to join the ballet.
He slipped and he slid, oh what a sight,
Dancing under the sun with all his might.

The waves went crash, the tide did tease,
While fishermen sang their off-key pleas.
A fish jumped high, in a twisty flip,
Wishing he'd brought along a script.

The sun made jokes, in rays so bright,
Tickling toes that were lost in flight.
A dog in sunglasses chased a sea plume,
While kids in buckets made their own room.

And as the day turned into a dream,
The stars blinked down, a playful beam.
On sunlit shores, where laughter flows,
In a lullaby of giggles and toes.

A Dance of Palm Fronds

Palm fronds whispered secrets to the breeze,
Inviting all critters for a little tease.
A squirrel in a hat led the parade,
While a tortoise grooved, not afraid.

Beneath a coconut tree's grand embrace,
A party erupted; oh, what a place!
The frogs in tuxes sang a sweet tune,
As donkeys attempted a wobbly swoon.

With each gust of wind, the leaves did sway,
In silly formations that danced away.
A snake hopped in, with a shimmy and shake,
Declaring the great palm dance a mistake!

But laughter erupted, no one cared,
For all were united, fully ensnared.
In a whirl of joy, the night was long,
As palm fronds echoed the island's song.

Warm Winds of Paradise

A parrot wearing shades flew by with ease,
Quipping to the seas, "Hey, feel that tease?"
A breeze so warm, it made fish giggle,
As dolphins danced in a merry wiggle.

On a picnic blanket, ants had a feast,
While a crab declared himself the king at least.
With forks made of shells, they cheered in delight,
Though the lemonade spilled, what a wild sight!

The sun offered sunscreen from a golden jar,
While the iguana strummed like a rockstar.
Warm winds whispered tales of cheer and fun,
As sandcastles crumbled, their time was done.

In this land of warmth, where laughter's spun,
Every grain of sand holds a story to run.
Through warm winds of joy, life's no riddle,
As each little moment can't help but twiddle.

Laughter in the Wind

The wind tells jokes as it rustles the leaves,
Where every giggle is sewn into weaves.
A monkey threw coconuts for fun,
While parrots cheered, "Let's go on the run!"

Fish wearing hats formed a swimming crew,
They sped through waves, yelling, "Look at you!"
An octopus juggled when the coast was clear,
Dropping his catch, then roaring with cheer.

A crab with a mustache flexed his hard shell,
As he pinched the breeze and claimed he was swell.
Laughter erupted, bouncing on high,
Carried like whispers into the sky.

In this animated realm, no one frowns,
As fun rides the currents, swirling 'round towns.
With laughter in the wind, it's clear to see,
Every day's a fiesta, wild and free!

Meadows of the Sea

Waves giggle as they tumble down,
Fish wear sunglasses, laughing in town.
Seagulls compete in a dance of grace,
Crabs throw a party, what a wild place!

Sandcastles wobble, feeling quite bold,
A turtle DJ spins tales of old.
Beach balls bounce, knocking folks about,
Laughter erupts, there's never a doubt!

Sunscreen battles—sticky delight,
Bikini-clad squirrels steal the show right.
Seashells gossip, whispering glee,
In this meadow, we're all truly free!

So come join the fun, don't stay inside,
With the waves, let's take a comical ride.
Splashes and giggles, all in good cheer,
In meadows of water, joy is quite near!

Leaves that Whisper Secrets

Palm fronds chatter with a rustling sound,
While ants play cards right there on the ground.
Tropical flowers wear hats oh so bright,
As breezes swirl in a comical flight.

Monkeys juggle coconuts high,
While parakeets mimic—it's worth a try!
An iguana struts, sporting a grin,
As the sun melts away, let the fun begin!

Fruit bats giggle, swinging from trees,
While crickets hum silly tunes with ease.
A sloth winks slowly, taking his time,
In the leafy whispers, everything's rhyme!

So grab a hat, join the joyful crew,
Where secrets of laughter swirl just for you.
In the breeze, listen close for the cheer,
As leaves share their tales, drawing you near!

Legends of the Calm Waters

Fish in tuxedos bob up in style,
As dolphins dance, adding to the mile.
Rumors spread through the water's cool swirl,
Of mermaids who laugh with a flick of a pearl.

A crab with a top hat gives quite the speech,
While the octopus juggles—now that's a peach!
Turtles tell tall tales of treasures so grand,
With giggles and wiggles, it's all quite unplanned.

Underwater mimosas create quite a stir,
Where seaweed dips low, and fish start to purr.
The moonlight dances, casting shadows that tease,
With legends of fun floating out in the breeze!

So dive into laughter, let worries just drift,
In calm water caverns, where humor's a gift.
Each splash brings a tale to recount at the shore,
In these legends we cherish, who could ask for more?

Daydreams in the Coastal Wind

Kites soar high with a whimsical twist,
While toddlers giggle, oh, how they insist!
The surf sings songs of childhood delight,
In daydreams of sandcastles, hearts feel light.

A pelican swoops, eyeing snacks with a wink,
As surfboards and belly-flops blur in a blink.
Sun hats are spinning like tops in a race,
While sandy toes dance at a ridiculous pace.

Ice cream drips, colors bright and surreal,
A parade of flavors—now that's a big deal!
Seashells are traded for giggles and fun,
With laughter in undertows—oh, what a run!

So swirl in the breeze, let your cares take flight,
In daydreams of coastal wonder, pure delight.
Come join the festivities, there's so much to see,
In the wind, we find joy—come sail wild and free!

Breezy Escapes in Paradise

With sandals flapping, we dance on sand,
A rush of laughter, just take my hand.
Palm trees whisper secrets, all in jest,
Join the beach party, feel truly blessed.

Each wave a giggle, a splash, a cheer,
Seagulls waddle by, give a sly leer.
Ice cream drips down, oh what a sight,
While sunburned noses gleam in the light.

The beach ball bounces, pops on a throw,
Rolls to a crab's home, is it friend or foe?
We chase after it, a messy parade,
In this sandy utopia, mischief is made.

As sunset approaches, we roast marshmallows,
Nature laughs with us, how sweet are the fellows.
With giggles and joy, our hearts grow bold,
In this breezy escape, memories unfold.

Kisses from the Warm Winds

Warm winds tickle my sun-kissed face,
A lazy hammock calls me to embrace.
Tropical fruits scatter on the ground,
As laughter and giggles are happily found.

Breezes carry whispers, a cheeky tease,
Coconuts rolling, oh what a breeze!
Flip-flops flop, and I trip on my toe,
In this windblown laughter, I'm free to flow.

Dancing with shadows beneath leafy shade,
Fruits turning into snacks, how sweetly delayed.
Silly selfies with crabs, oh what a sight,
In this sun-drenched chaos, everything feels right.

The warm winds chuckle, as day turns to night,
Stars pop out, ready to twinkle and bite.
With whispers of fun that never will end,
In these kisses of warmth, we lose and we blend.

Island Heartbeat

Here on this island, my heart skips a beat,
Sand between toes, oh such a treat!
The sun's golden rays bring a goofy grin,
While sea turtles laugh, let the fun begin!

The rhythm of waves hums a silly tune,
Crabs strut with swagger, under the moon.
We play hide-and-seek with the ocean spray,
In this lively heart dance, come join the fray!

My coconut hat flies away with the breeze,
Chasing its shadow, oh please, don't tease!
We run hand in hand, like kids on the shore,
With laughter erupting, who could ask for more?

As night wraps us up, twinkling stars cheer,
Coconut dreams whisper, sweet nothings here.
With giggles and joy, the island beats strong,
In this playful heart, we forever belong.

Sailor's Soliloquy under Stars

On a boat, I swab with a mop made of dreams,
While fish tease my cap, or so it seems.
The stars wink down, with a mischievous air,
As I sing off-key, without a care.

The wind plays tricks, tugs at my beard,
Each wave a chuckle, as sailors are cheered.
Clouds drift by, sharing laughter so sweet,
In this quirky voyage, life can't be beat.

Seashells collect stories, with each tide's kiss,
While I barter with gulls, oh what bliss!
With fishy companions I build my tale,
Sailing through antics, we blow wind in sail.

By starlit lanterns, tonight's mischief lies,
The crew rolls in laughter, under vast skies.
With a smile and a wink, let our tales spin,
In this sailor's soliloquy, fun's sure to win.

Breezes from Blissful Palms

A gentle sway, a wobbly dance,
A coconut lands, oh what a chance!
It rolls with a giggle, down to my feet,
Who knew a nut could be so sweet?

The sun in the sky, it starts to frown,
As I chase that rogue nut all over town!
With sandy toes and a goofy grin,
It's hard not to laugh when you fall in!

Squirrels and birds join in the chase,
As the coconut rolls, what a funny race!
With palm leaves waving, cheering out loud,
Who knew this coconut could gather a crowd?

Finally caught, I sit on the sand,
With a coconut hat, looking rather grand!
A breeze picks up, laughter fills the air,
Oh the joy found in this nutty affair!

Hidden Oasis Lullaby

In a secret spot, where the palm trees hum,
A coconut dream is about to come.
I lay down to nap, just one little snooze,
But that nut has other plans, oh how I loose!

It rolls off my head and starts to sing,
A little coconut with a laugh and a swing.
I chase it around, my sleepy eyes wide,
What fun in the shade, what a silly ride!

With each twist and turn, it drums on my back,
A nutty symphony, no time to slack!
The breeze whispers secrets from the trees,
As I tumble and giggle with grace like a breeze.

Wrapped in the laughter of lazy delight,
Who would have thought a nut could take flight?
With friends in the leaves, and a giggling spree,
Life's simple joys bring sweet jubilee!

Sunlit Fronds and Shadows

Sunlight dances on the coconut shell,
I thought it was empty, but boy, can it yell!
It rolled on the ground, doing flips and tricks,
As I watched in delight, feeling all of its kicks.

Shade from the palm, where mischief begins,
That nut has got plans for some silly spins.
It giggles and hops, in its own little way,
Making the sun jealous, come out to play!

With shadows that stretch and laughter that gleams,
Coconuts plotting their nutty schemes.
The breeze has a chuckle, as waves pull and weave,
In a dance with the palm fronds, we hold our reprieve.

A nut rumbles loudly, it's taking the lead,
Who knew such a fruit could be so full of speed?
I run with delight, can't catch it today,
Yet here in the sun, I find joy in the play!

Warm Embrace of the Sea

Down by the shore, where the waves kiss the sand,
A coconut rolls in, I can't understand!
With warmth of the sun, it starts to glide,
What strange little dramas this nut does decide!

It jumps in the waves, yelling "Cannonball!"
I'm doubled with laughter, oh what a call!
It splashes the seagulls, making them squawk,
With each silly wave, it's a nutty talk!

The breeze pulls me closer as giggles ensue,
That rogue little fruit, always plotting its coup.
A sea breeze delivers this playful surprise,
As I stumble and trip, with bright, sparkling eyes.

The sun melts away with a chuckle tonight,
As the coconut leaves on its magical flight.
With warmth in our hearts and laughter so free,
Who knew a nut could bring such glee?

Symphony of Coastal Skies

Seagulls dance in sunlit air,
A coconut does not seem to care.
With a grin, it rolls away,
Joining the fun in its own ballet.

Sandy toes and laughter loud,
We chase our hats, the breeze so proud.
A beach ball bounces, oh so high,
While sunburned folks let out a sigh.

Mellow Hours beneath the Palm

Lazy days with ice cream cones,
The palm trees sway with silly tones.
A squirrel ponders, looking wise,
While tourists take their selfies, shy.

Chilling under leafy shade,
Thoughts of snacks, we're unafraid.
A rumble rolls, which stomach?
A feast awaits, so well we chuck!

Island Whispers

Whispers float on salty air,
Rumors of a hidden heir.
Coconuts with pirates plan,
To take a trip, just them and Stan.

Laughter echoes by the shore,
As clumsy crabs wage their war.
Flip-flops flying left and right,
"Oh, got sand in my drink!"—what a sight!

Fragrant Tropic Drift

A scent of fruit is in the breeze,
Chasing seagulls with all my keys.
Limes and giggles all around,
Causing mischief, joy unbound.

Umbrellas up, drinks in hand,
Toasting to this merry land.
Sipping slowly, tales unfold,
Of jests and splashes, purest gold.

www.ingramcontent.com/pod-product-compliance
Lightning Source LLC
Chambersburg PA
CBHW072121070526
44585CB00016B/1520